Cognitive Behavioral Therapy

I0429046

A Practical Guide To C.B.T. For Overcoming Anxiety, Depression, Addictions & Other Psychological Conditions

Jane Aniston

Introduction

If you have ever had to cope with a mental health condition that has caused your quality life to suffer, and relief was not available via a regular visit to the doctor's office or through taking medication, you'll know what it is like to feel powerless. Such is the reality of people living with anxiety, depression and the various mental health disorders. Mental illnesses usually start as negative thought patterns in the mind, and gradually manifest into debilitating physiological symptoms that can eventually cause a myriad of problems in one's life. The key to treating mental disorders lies in getting to the root cause of the problem; namely, identifying the thoughts, behaviors, experiences and other accumulated factors that led to a person developing the disorder in the first place.

Thankfully, there has been an increasing amount of attention given to mental illnesses within the medical field in the past half a decade or so. With more awareness being raised about the long-term dangers of poor mental health, great strides have been made in the development of treatment methods. One of the most commonly administered treatments for mental conditions that has been proven effective is Cognitive Behavioral Therapy (CBT).

Basically, CBT is a form of psychotherapy where patients work with a qualified therapist to identify negative thoughts and harmful behavioral patterns, and then learn how to respond positively to their problems, ultimately breaking free from the vicious cycle that is causing their suffering.

The beauty of CBT is that it can work just as effectively as a self-help method, provided that one is willing to learn the basic techniques, and then apply what they have learnt in their daily lives to improve their own situation. CBT is not just for managing mental disorders though; its techniques – as you will soon learn – can be employed to help in dealing with stress, helping one sleep better, and even eat a more healthy diet.

This guide cuts right to the chase by introducing the core principles of CBT in the first chapter, explaining how the therapy works, and what you can do to get started. In the subsequent chapters we will dive into the step-by-step process of conducting your own self-help therapy with basic CBT techniques. Each chapter is a crucial step in the entire process, so take your time and patiently work through each chapter, and make sure you have a firm grasp of the concepts and techniques before moving on. You will also find bolded sentences throughout the book; these are important points to take note of which include calls to action which you should be sure to act on as you work your way through the program.

One last thing must be made clear before you begin: while CBT is a fantastic method to help with changing our thoughts and behavioral patterns, it is not a miracle, overnight cure to all your problems. You will learn to deconstruct whatever issues you are facing, and deal with them positively rather than letting them take over your life. With CBT, you will have the tools

to take back the reigns and regain control of your life.

Table of contents

Chapter 1

Cognitive Behavioral Therapy Explained

What makes cognitive behavioral therapy (CBT) so effective in treating mental disorders is the therapy's simple and easily applied principles, which merge fundamental concepts in philosophy, behavioral therapy and cognitive therapy. It is often the preferred method for mental healthcare professionals and patients, because of the practicality and immediacy of its techniques in helping to identify and resolve problems. CBT also generally requires fewer sessions, compared to other types of therapy.

The following are some of the mental health conditions that can be treated with CBT:

- Anxiety disorders

- Clinical depression

- Sleep disorders

- Sexual disorders

- Phobias

- Eating disorders

- Substance abuse and dependency

- Post-traumatic stress disorder (PTSD)

- Obsessive-compulsive disorder (OCD)

- Schizophrenia

Despite its widespread use in the treatment of numerous mental disorders, CBT is also a useful tool that can help anyone better manage the emotional challenges in various life situations. In fact, it can help people deal with their problems for improved overall well-being, *before* those troubling emotions escalate into health issues. If you are not currently suffering with a mental health condition, here are some of the ways in which you can still use CBT techniques to improve your life:

- Managing stress

- Managing strong, overwhelming emotions like anger, grief and fear

- Overcoming personality weaknesses and gaining more confidence

- Overcoming emotional trauma from prior bad experiences

- Resolving relationship conflict and improving communication

- Dealing with distress arising from coping with a chronic medical condition

- Managing chronic physical symptoms, such as pain, sleeplessness and fatigue

How it Works

In a nutshell, CBT is concerned with two things:

- How you think about yourself, the world, other people and the events that happen around you

- How your actions affect your thoughts and feelings

CBT works on the fundamental principle that how we feel is not the result of what happened to us, but rather how we react to those events. In other words, your emotions are influenced by the meanings you attach to an object, person, event or situation. Shakespeare aptly sums up this theory in the quote, "There is nothing either good or bad but thinking makes it so."

Consider this: you saw an acquaintance at a social function and she did not come over to say hi. Now, there are several ways you can interpret this situation whereby your response could indicate an underlying problem:

a) You think that she is avoiding you like everyone else because nobody likes you (low self-esteem, could be emotional sign of depression).

b) You hope she doesn't notice or approach you, because you are worried that you may say or do something to embarrass yourself (symptoms of social anxiety).

c) You think she is just snotty (anger from overreaction).

d) Maybe she just didn't see you because she was busy entertaining others, but that's okay because you'll catch up with her later (the healthy response).

CBT can help a person make changes in the way they think (cognitive) and the way they act (behavior), by drawing a link between thoughts, feelings and actions.

You will learn to see the clear picture of the problem you are struggling with, so that you can begin to break your problems down into manageable chunks. Then, you will learn the skills necessary to change your destructive thoughts and behavioral patterns, thus helping you feel better and free from the vicious cycle of negativity.

For instance, when someone who suffers from social anxiety is invited to a gathering, they may think, "I don't know a lot of the people there. I could end up saying or doing something wrong, and they will laugh at me." Such thoughts will make the person feel irrationally anxious, prompting them to avoid the event. In isolation, their fear of being judged and ridiculed grows stronger, causing them to shy away from socializing even more. This is how a vicious cycle begins.

With the help of CBT, the socially anxious individual would start by identifying the problematic thought-emotion-action connection. Once the problem is clearly defined, they can then learn new skills to work towards feeling better. In the given example, the person could make an effort to attend more small social gatherings. They will also learn to question their unfounded worries about being judged by others.

How to Make CBT Work for You

CBT techniques are very structured, easy to follow and perfectly safe for anyone with mild to moderate mental health disorders, and even those who are simply looking to resolve emotionally challenging issues in life. There is substantial research that shows CBT to be just as effective as medication for the treatment of mental conditions, and it also works well in combination with medication. Moreover, the therapy is also a good alternative for cases where medication is not a viable option, such as when a patient is pregnant or on other prescription drugs.

While it is helpful to look to the past to understand how it has influenced your life and may have given rise to problems, CBT mostly focuses on the present and finding the solutions to improve your overall well-being at this moment in time. As you work through each successive step, whether with a therapist or on your own, you can successfully manage the signs and symptoms of mental illnesses and prevent future relapses.

In essence, CBT is guided self-help. The ultimate aim of is for the patient to be independent of therapy, and incorporate the skills they have learnt into their daily lives until it becomes habitual. The true benefit comes from minimizing or stopping one's problems even after the therapy's duration is over.

Become Your Own Therapist

To reap, you need to commit yourself to the process. There is vitally important if you wish to see meaningful results. Even if you enlist the help of a therapist, they cannot make your problems go away without your full co-operation. Generally, anyone can be their own therapist with CBT. However, self-help therapy may not be suitable for people with more complex mental health issues or learning difficulties.

If you are ready to begin using CBT techniques, the following chapters offer a four-step program that will take you by the hand, and help you work through whatever issues you are struggling with. All you have to do is follow each step closely; do not gloss over any of the steps, and always do your homework by taking the appropriate action and practicing what you have learnt.

Chapter 2

Identifying The Vicious Cycle

To begin your own self-help CBT, all you will need is a journal in which you can write down your progress. Throughout this program, you will be given two examples – social anxiety (a mental disorder) and low self-esteem (a common problem) – to better demonstrate how the techniques described can be applied. Study the examples for better understanding, and then feel free to adapt the techniques to suit the needs of your own individual situation.

Drawing the Big Picture

To start off, you will identify the thoughts, feelings and behaviors that are keeping your problems going – the vicious cycle of negativity. **Make the first entry in your CBT journal by writing down lists for the following five areas:**

- **What is the problem you're experiencing?** Think about what is causing you distress; be it an event, situation or group of people. If you have been diagnosed with a mental disorder by a doctor, you will know the underlying cause of the issues you are tackling. Note down anything you believe will be helpful – time, place, people, incidents etc.

- **What thoughts or images were going through your mind at that time?** Think about what ran through your head at the time; what did those thoughts mean to you? What does it say about you or the situation? What bothers you? Do you have unanswered questions that feel unsettling?

- **How did you feel?** Describe your emotions; did you feel hurt, anger, resentment, disturbed, fear, worry or depressed?

- **What did you notice about your body?** With every thought, a chemical reaction in the brain will follow, triggering some sort of physical response. In cases of intense, overwhelming emotions, a physical response may be overpowering and debilitating. Furthermore, thoughts and feelings associated with a mental disorder can create a number of physiological symptoms. Hence, it is important to pay attention to what your body goes through. Take note of any uncomfortable sensations and when they occur, such as irregular heartbeat, difficulty breathing, trembling, lightheadedness, lethargy and stomach discomfort etc. Note down also the less obvious physical reactions, including low sex drive, feeling unusually awake at night, loss of appetite and indigestion.

- **What did you do?** How did you react to the troubling situation? What is your own method of coping with the distressing thoughts, feelings and physical symptoms?

Once you have completed your journal entry, you will have a bird's eye view of what you have been going through. This will act as a 'roadmap' in your journey towards treating the problem. **Do not rush this process; take as much time as you need, and make your entries as long and detailed as you deem necessary to achieve a thorough understanding. You may want to do this a few times, over the course of several days and weeks to see if a pattern emerges.**

Example 1: Social Anxiety

Feeling anxious is normal when you are responding to an unfamiliar situation or or faced with danger. In such situations, the body's fight-or-flight response kicks in, sending an adrenal rush to the bloodstream and creating a sense of urgency that translates into a racing heartbeat, sweating, trembling, rapid breathing and an impending sense of doom. This is our primal survival mechanism at work, and it works without fail whether the perceived danger is real or not. When the impending threat is over, one's emotional and physiological state will return to being calm.

However, when our anxious feelings are intense and uncontrollable, to the point of interfering with our ordinary day-to-day activities, it is a sign of an anxiety disorder. People who suffer from an anxiety disorder feel overblown, often unfounded worries and fears occupying their thoughts and giving rise to uncomfortable physiological symptoms. As stated, the example given here is concerned with an anxiety disorder, so feel free to adapt the process learnt to help overcome whatever situation is making you feel nervous, depressed, negative or just uncomfortable.

The following is an example journal entry for a person suffering from an anxiety disorder, specifically known as social anxiety or social phobia:

Situation:

Was tasked with giving a presentation on the company's latest products at a trade fair next week.

Thoughts:

- I don't think I can pull it off.

- My colleagues will laugh at me.

- What if I mess it up? The boss will be so angry; I'm going to get scolded, humiliated and lose my job.

Feelings:

Worry, fear (of embarrassment), doubt and restlessness

Physical sensations:

* Heart palpitations, accompanied by profuse sweating and rapid breathing that occur unexpectedly during the day – especially when the assignment is being discussed.

* Haven't had a peaceful 8-hour sleep for the past three nights; feeling tired during the day and also don't feel like eating much.

What did I do?

* Avoid people at the office as best as possible, especially those who keep bringing up the subject.

* Leave work early to be alone at home.

* Try not to think about the presentation.

Example 2: Low Self-Esteem

Whether we care to admit or not, we live in a critical world where people tend to evaluate themselves and others according to a certain scale we hold in our minds. Self-esteem comes from the value a person perceives themselves to have. If you get into the habit of thinking negatively about yourself, the result will be low self-esteem – a belief that you are not good enough, and that you do not matter as much as others.

Low self-esteem can also be the result of life experiences that have caused us to question our sense of worth, especially during a time when we were young and impressionable. For example, a person who was bullied, abused, criticized, put down or judged negatively will likely think less of themselves.

Having low self-esteem is generally not a mental illness, although it can have a very real impact on one's life. However, if negative self-criticism is allowed to persist, one may be at risk of developing an anxiety disorder or depression.

Here is a sample CBT journal entry for a person trying to deal with their low self-esteem:

Situation:

I feel out of place at my new job. I have trouble interacting and getting along with others. I also often wonder if my performance is good enough, or if I could do better.

Thoughts:

- It must be me; I'm just not fun to be around with.

- Maybe I should change the way I dress and act.

- I should have joined my co-workers for drinks after hours more often; though frankly, I prefer a quiet evening at home than going to the bar.

- I should have spoken up about the idea I had at yesterday's meeting. Not speaking up was a mistake!

- What would happen if suggest a new place to go for lunch together?

Feelings:

Frustrated, lonely, depressed, dejected, nervous and regretful

Physical sensations:

None in particular, although I do tend to stutter when I'm nervous.

What did I do?

- I pretended to like the TV series everyone was talking about; helps me blend in.

- Put in extra hours at work – hopefully it will help me get a head of other, and perhaps they will notice and like me if I achieve something worthwhile.

- Explain that I can't join them for drinks after work because I have other things to do at home.

- Agree to do favors for others more often, even if I'm not really up to it.

Chapter 3

Making Behavioral Changes

The first step required to remedy a problem is to change how we react when confronted with a distressing situation. Just as the way we think and feel can trigger physical responses, our behavior can greatly affect the way we think and feel.

Go back to what you wrote about your vicious cycles; pay particular attention to what you wrote down in regards to 'behaviors'. We usually act automatically when under stress without thinking about the consequences of our actions. **Looking at what you are used to doing to cope with your problems, make an objective assessment by answering these questions as honestly as possible and writing down your responses:**

- What helped me and get through the things that are causing me distress?

- What actions did I actually take?

- What did I avoid doing?

- What automatic reactions am I prone to having?

- What were the consequences of my actions?

- Did it affect the way I feel later, and if so, how?

Work toward Solutions

Having assessed your behaviors, ask yourself the following:

- What could I have done differently?

- What would someone else have done in that situation? (think about particular people that you know, and what they might have done differently)

- Have there been times in the past when I would have done something else?

- If I had paused, and taken the time to think about the situation carefully, what would I have done?

Give yourself time to think of several options to what you may have done differently, and write them all down as they occur to you. After you have finished, ask yourself:

- If I had tried that, how different would the situation have turned out?

- How would it have affected the way I felt?

- How would it have affected what I thought?

- Would it have been more helpful or effective for me? How would it have affected other people or the overall situation?

- What would the consequences have been if I'd have behaved differently?

Formulate an Action Plan

When you find yourself in a distressing situation, simply taking a breather and stepping away from the problem can help you assess the situation more clearly, and make better decision on how to respond. **To break a vicious cycle, you need to substitute destructive behaviors with sensible and positive actions.** That is easier said than done though! However, with proper thought and planning, using what you have been journaling so far, you can start making changes in your daily life and building good habits that go a long way to keeping the negative vicious cycle from recurring.

Now, think about healthy and realistic options for dealing with distressing emotions to replace your usual behaviors. This is your personal action plan, so choose what works best for you. Write down a list of things you can do, and as you go along, ask yourself the following:

- What are the best and most helpful solutions for my situation?

- How will it help out with my problems?

- Will this/these option/s be effective and appropriate?

- Is it practical in terms of the particular event?

- Does it align with my personal beliefs, values and principles?

- What consequences will it have in my day-to-day life?

- How will it affect my normal daily routine?

- Will others around me be involved or affected?

- By doing this, am I just avoiding my problems?

When making your action plan, you want to be mindful that your choice of activities is not a way of denying and avoiding your problems, because that will only worsen the situation. **Whatever you resist will persist! The key is to find activities that will keep your thoughts occupied and make you feel better; not a temporary escapism for your troubles.** This means you may need to think about confronting your fears, work on kicking a bad habit or carrying out a "lifestyle overhaul", if that is what it takes to improve your well-being. Here are some suggestions of activities that can help pull us out of the self-destructive loop:

- Teach yourself to pause and take deep breaths rather than responding impulsively

- Relaxation techniques, such as deep breathing, visualization, yoga, meditation and prayer

- Grounding techniques, like touching something tangible, hold a comforting object, and surround yourself with familiar sounds, scent and sights

- Stay connected to trusted friends and family, so that you will always have someone to talk to about your problems

- Start a physical exercise routine

- Take up a creative endeavor – painting, learn a new music instrument, take a creative writing course or redecorate your house

- Pamper yourself; go for a massage, watch a movie, treat yourself to a nice dinner and go shopping (within your means, of course)

- Cultivate a positive inner voice; encourage yourself with affirmations like "I can do this!", "I'll be okay, this will come to pass", "I'm strong enough to go through this", "I've been through this before and I can do it again!" and "I'm better than that!" – make these self-motivating affirmations your personal mantras

Just Do It!

A plan is only any good if it is actually being implemented. So, after you have your plan clearly charted out, then the obvious next step is to follow through on it. Let us be realistic, making lasting behavioral changes will not happen overnight. It will take some time for old habits to die and be replaced by new positive behaviors.

Don't set yourself up for failure. Just make an effort to start with small baby steps by doing something different to what you normally would each day, as only do as much as you can comfortably manage. As long as you are doing something – however small it may be – it's a step in the right direction. Start small and stay consistent; slowly, like a rolling snowball, your accumulated efforts will change your life for the better.

Example 1: Social Anxiety

What I usually do?

- Avoid people at the office as best as possible, especially those who keep bringing up the subject of presentation and public speaking.

- Leave work early to be alone at home.

- Try not to think about and avoid social situations that feels like all eyes are on me.

- Eat lunch alone in my cubicle.

Action Plan:

- Make an effort to join in on discussions and speak up (a way to face up to my fears).

- At least once a week, join colleague for after hours outing, or as someone to join me for dinner.

- Meet up with friends for a catch-up session at least once a month on Saturday.

- Eat lunch at the office cafeteria, and eat out every Tuesdays and Thursdays just to be around people.

- Join hip hop dance class and just have fun.

Example 1: Low Self-Esteem

What I usually do?

- I pretended to like the TV series everyone was talking about; helps me blend in.

- Put in extra hours at work – hopefully it will help me get a head of other, and perhaps they will notice and like me if I achieve something worthwhile.

- Explain that I can't join them for drinks after work because I have other things to do at home, when I actually don't.

- Agree to do favors for others more often, even if I'm not really up to it.

Action Plan:

- Get into the habit of saying what I mean, regardless of how other may feel – because my opinions matter.

- Leave the office on time; go for a movie every other Wednesday and get a massage on payday, maybe stop by my favorite clothing store and see what's new.

- Join friends for drinks, but go for non-alcohol option.

- Get into the habit of saying no to things I don't want to do without having to explain myself in detail.

- Tell myself one positive thing about me every morning before heading out to work.

Chapter 4

Change The Way You Think

As humans, we are creatures of habit. Whether we care to admit it or are aware of it, we get into the habit of thinking in particular ways, as influenced by our individual life experiences, which includes upbringing, culture and education. Our life experiences shaped the way we make sense of the world around us and the way we react to the situations we find ourselves in.

You may think that it is impossible to escape our customary way of thinking; that we have no control over our thoughts. It is certainly true that we cannot easily stop or control the things that pop into our mind. However, thoughts are not necessarily true, nor are they always helpful. Whatever you do, a thought is going to follow because they are generated as automatic messages from the brain. What we can do though, is choose how we react to them. Hence, when negative thoughts creep up, we can learn to react to them differently

You have learnt how to change your behavior towards distressing situations. It is now time to look once again at your vicious cycle notes, and look at how you thoughts influence how you feel and act.

Don't Be Bullied!

To truly understand how our thoughts can work against us and how we can change that, let's examine the playground bully metaphor. A typical school playground has high fencing to make it a safe place where children can not wander off from, and outsiders cannot trespass. The safety feature, however, does not keep the children in the playground safe from the bully – that troublesome mean kid who picks on other kids in school.

Now, consider the following situations of three bullying victims and how the bully would react to each one:

- **Victim 1:** Gets hurled insults by the bully, becomes upset and runs off crying. How do you think the bully would react? He would probably enjoy it and will likely carry on targeting this kid for his own amusement.

- **Victim 2:** Gets insulted by the bully, yet remains unfazed, and then responds with a smart rebuttal. The bully is taken aback, but he will probably have another go and yell back. The two kids might carry on, trading insults, but the bully will eventually get tired and leave this victim alone.

- **Victim 3:** Hears the bully's mean words, looks at him in acknowledgement, but doesn't react at all and instead goes off to play with his friends. The bully's reaction? No fun to be had here, might as well give up.

As you can see from the three scenarios, there are different ways to respond to something and each would trigger a different consequence. **Imagine your negative thoughts as your own inner bully.** When you believe your thoughts (the bully), you allow them to dictate how you feel and behave, and those thoughts will keep on coming (like Victim 1). You can challenge your own thoughts (Victim 2) by checking to see if they have any basis in reality, and you will then think carefully before allowing them to influence your emotions and actions. Finally, if you just acknowledge your thoughts, choose not to believe them, and then direct your attention elsewhere, they will have no bearing on how you feel and act.

Are you stuck in a situation similar to that of Victim 1, where your negative thoughts have a hold on you, causing you to stay trapped in a vicious cycle of negative emotions? If so, you are now ready to break free from them by learning to do what Victim 2 did when bullied.

Question Your Thoughts

Look back at the thoughts that ran through you mind during a distressing situation. You may write down a few more from recent events. Of all of these thoughts, which one thought (or mental image) contributed most to making you feel upset? You will now put that thought under a 'microscope' and analyze it by asking the following questions. Feel free to repeat this process as many times as you feel necessary for noted thoughts that trigger strong emotions. Be sure to note down your responses:

- Is this thought a fact, or is it in reality, baseless?

- What am I really reacting to?

- What meaning am I giving this situation?

- Is there another way of looking at it?

- What would someone else make of it? (It's often helpful to think about a particular person who you respect – even if it is a celebrity or fictional character – and imagine what they would think about that thought, what meaning they would give it, and what they would do.)

- What advice would I give someone else with this thought, if they were in my situation?

- Is this one of those unhelpful thinking habits?

- Am I just overreacting?

- How important is this really? How important will it be in a few years time?

- How am I reacting?

- If I try to see this situation as an outside observer, what would it look like? Would things appear to have a different meaning?

- Can I be more flexible in my thinking?

- What evidence is there that this thought is true?

- What evidence is there that this thought isn't true?

- What would be a more balanced way of looking at it?

- What is the bigger picture, and what does this thought mean in the grand scheme of things?

Defusing Harmful Thoughts

Remember the playground bully's Victim 3? Unlike the other two victims, Victim 3 chooses to acknowledge the bully, and then turn his focus towards playing with his friends. Defusing harmful thoughts involves acknowledging them (what you resist will persist, remember?), not reacting automatically, and then choosing to focus elsewhere.

When you are able to arrive at this state of mind, negative thoughts that would once trigger a reaction be mean nothing more than passing ideas. You will no longer unquestioningly accept them as truths. Learning to distance and defuse negative thoughts is far from easy though. It will require your diligence, patience, and persistent effort, but the more you keep practicing, the easier it will get.

Now we have looked at the idea of challenging our negative thoughts, let's begin rendering them ineffective by asking these questions:

- What thoughts, feelings and sensations do I notice (now that I have questioned my thoughts, rather than accepting them for truths)?

- What exactly is it that I am I reacting to?

- What meaning am I attaching to this event and how is that affecting me?

- What is the result of my believing this thought?

- What would be the effect of not believing this thought?

- Am I just predicting what might happen in the future based on how I feel (with no reasonable or factual basis)?

- Is this connected to a memory from the past?

- Is this one of those unhelpful thinking habits?

As you begin making a conscious choice to not engage with your negative thoughts, it may be easy to be distracted by factors that will reel you back to them. You can practice a simple mindfulness breathing technique to help anchor your thought to the present moment. Whenever you notice you mind wandering, take slow, deep breaths and bring your attention back to your breathing. If you are engaged in an activity as a distraction, bring your focus back to it and away from thoughts that threaten you inner peace.

Example 1: Social Anxiety

Thought: People are going to make fun of what I say or do.

How will I know if this is really the case? Have I ever been humiliated in the past? Why do I have to worry about what others think? Even if it is true, it should not matter, because come to think of it, nothing much has changed in my life. I still have friends who enjoy my company and a job that I am good at. I know this to be true because I have been working in the same company for three years now, and the boss has entrusted me with doing presentations for clients. I have successfully pulled them off before, so why should I let them linger in my mind? I notice that I often lose sleep for days leading up to and after a public speaking event.

So, what if I did or say something wrong? What is the worst that could happen? I suppose I can just sincerely apologize for it and laugh it off. If I were to be scolded for it, I will have to own up to my mistakes, because that's what I would advise, if someone in a sticky situation asked.

Example 2: Low Self-Esteem

Thought: I feel like nobody likes me. Maybe I'm not fun to hang out with because I don't share a lot of the interests as most people of my age.

Is this just my imagination? I don't have any real proof that it is true, after all. When was the last time I joined a group of friends to do something fun? I went out for coffee with some old school mates, and we had fun. They laughed along with me and we recount memories.

Every time I keep thinking that people don't like to be around me, it makes me hesitate to call up my friends and make plans. I don't like going to pubs and karaoke, and there is nothing wrong with that. I'll have to find other common ground with my friends.

Chapter 5

Practice Makes Perfect

As mentioned at the beginning of this book, CBT is not a magical therapy that will whisk your troubles away. It takes hard work and commitment, but the difference it can make in your life will be worth the time and effort.

If you have been following each step of this guide, you are well on your way to making effective positive changes in your life. To ensure you really benefit from this program, you need to keep practicing the techniques that you have learnt. **Refer back to your CBT journal as often as necessary to remind yourself of your action plan and the techniques you need to keep practicing. Make a note of how you feel, think and behave as you go along; this will be a record of your progress.**

To track your progress, make it a point – once a month will do – to sit down and peruse your journal. Look at early entries and compare them to more recent entries to see how far you have come. Think about the following questions as you evaluate your progress:

- What have you learned that has been the most helpful?

- What hasn't helped and what can you do differently?

- What has helped and how can you improve on it?

- What is worth continuing to practice?

- What can you do to help or remind yourself to practice regularly?

- What help do you need and how can you find it?

After some time, you will not need to write things down as much as you used to as the techniques and skills you have been practicing will become habitual. With constant practice, you will find yourself practicing all the steps effortlessly and without prior planning. Before you know it, you will notice that your reality has become freer and happier.

Conclusion

I hope this book has given you a more thorough insight into the uses of CBT and it's viability as a solution for overcoming numerous psychological ailments.

By following the steps outlined in this book, you will be able to move forward into a more fulfilling future. Good luck, and remember, if in doubt seek help from a trained professional.

A message from the author

Finally, if you enjoyed this book, **please** take the time to post a review on Amazon. It will only take a couple of minutes and I'd be extremely grateful for your support.

Jane Aniston

FREE BONUS NUMBER 1!

As a free bonus, I've included a preview of one of my other best-selling books, "Overcoming Anxiety - Practical Approaches You Can Use To Manage Fear & Anxiety In The Moment & Long Term"!

ALSO...

be sure to check out my other books. Scroll to the back of this book for a list of other books written by me, along with download links.

Enjoy!

FREE BONUS!: Preview Of

"Overcoming Anxiety - Practical Approaches You Can Use To Manage Fear & Anxiety In The Moment & Long Term"

If you enjoyed this book, I have a little bonus for you; a preview of one of my other books "Overcoming Anxiety - Practical Approaches You Can Use To Manage Fear & Anxiety In The Moment & Long Term", which goes into more detail on how you can manage anxiety safely and naturally! Enjoy!

Lifestyle Changes for a Long-Term Solution

Overcoming anxiety over the long haul takes more than just a few quick fixes to quell the nerves; it requires making lifestyles changes. The changes that have to be made include getting more physically active, working on achieving optimal sleep patterns, learning to handle and minimize stress better, quitting (or at least heavily cutting down on) alcohol and smoking, cutting down on caffeinated beverages, and switching to a healthier eating habit. Long-term changes cannot happen overnight; it will require commitment and patience, as you gradually take realistic steps towards improving your mental and physical health.

Get More Active

Easily the most important and helpful thing you can incorporate into your life is a regular exercise routine. Living a sedentary lifestyle filled with stress will definitely contribute to more senseless worrying. On the other hand, frequent exercise has been proven in numerous studies to reduce anxiety symptoms. Your overall well-being will benefit due to exercise causing your body to release feel-good hormones and chemicals that will improve mood and promote relaxation.

If you have never exercised regularly in the past, you can start building the habit of being more active with simple activities that get you moving. Consider taking a 30-minute stroll around the neighborhood every morning before going to work, parking your car some distance from your destination and walking the rest of the way, taking the stairs over riding the escalator, going for a nature hike on the weekends or taking a longer than usual walk with your dog. Although these may seem like relatively minor steps, if you do them regularly you'll find yourself feeling more energized and building a higher level of self discipline. This in turn should not only allow you to move on to more strenuous exercise, but is also very likely to give you a mental boost and make you feel good about yourself.

Take Up a Formal Exercise Program

To obtain the full benefit of physical activity, consider allocating time for a formal exercise program. This involves a regular set of exercises which you have to take time out of your daily life for, such as lifting weights at the gym, attending an aerobics class, or taking up a sport. It can be challenging to commit yourself to exercising, especially when you have work-life demands to fulfill. That being said, where there is a will, there is definitely a way! Think of the money spent on health club memberships and time allocated to exercising as an investment in yourself, because your well-being matters. Again, the benefits of regular excursus have been proven by numerous studies to lead to HUGE benefits; some studies have even found that exercising regularly can be as effective as taking pharmaceutical drugs when combatting conditions such as anxiety and depression!

Try Yoga

A non-religious spiritual practice that originates from India thousands of years ago, yoga has often been touted as the comprehensive mind, body and spirit workout. These claims are far from an exaggeration though. Academic research in the western world since the 1970s has considered yoga one of the best possible treatments for depression and anxiety. Since the early 2000s, yoga has gained worldwide popularity as a fitness lifestyle practice, which has lead to it becoming a staple program offered in many gyms and health clubs. There are event studios and vacation retreats dedicated to the practice, offering courses to yogis of all levels.

In a nutshell, yoga is a system of exercise that comprises deep meditation, breathing techniques and series of physical workouts in the form of postures known as *Asana*. Some of the more orthodox yoga schools and teachers would even encourage students to incorporate the spiritual (but non-religious) elements of yoga. With consistent practice, one can reap the multiple benefits of yoga, which include:

- A calm, steady and equanimous mind

- Improved mood

- Hormonal balance

- Greater flexibility and range of motion

- Greater spinal and joint health

- Improved strength and muscle tone

- Steady weight loss and maintenance

- Lowered risk of sports injury

- Lowered risk of various chronic illnesses

- Improved self-confidence

- An overall brighter outlook on life

Those who are unfamiliar with yoga may be intimidated by the demonstration of postures that seem to require a vast amount of strength and flexibility. That should not deter you from trying out this transformative workout, because there are literally hundreds of yoga postures and they vary in difficulty. Moreover, a competent instructor – known as a guru – can guide a beginner through the practice, providing modifications to difficult postures, so the student can ease themselves into the practice.

The practice of yoga has a long history, which has branched into different traditions and styles. Certain styles are more suited to relaxation, whereas some are more physically demanding. If you intend to begin practicing yoga, take time to choose a studio and teacher that offers the style of yoga best suited to your needs.

(Chapter 4 continues in the full book)

Cognitive Behavioral Therapy and Anxiety Disorders

Because anxiety disorders vary significantly in severity among sufferers, the treatment administered normally depends on each individual's case. One of the most common and renowned treatments for anxiety disorders is Cognitive Behavioral Therapy (CBT). It has been scientifically tested and found to be effective in hundreds of clinical trials for remedying many different mental disorders. Unlike other forms of psychotherapy, CBT is more problem-solving oriented. Patients learn specific skills that involve identifying distorted thinking patterns, modifying beliefs, relating to others differently and changing behaviors – skills which can be used for the rest of their lives.

This chapter will give you the basics on CBT, so that you will know what to expect from this treatment when seeking professional medical help for anxiety disorder.

The Theory Behind CBT

Simply put, CBT is based on the cognitive model of how the way we perceive things and situations can influence the way we feel and behave. In other words, if you interpret a situation negatively, you might feel negative emotions as a result and that in turn will lead you to behave in a certain manner. For example, someone who is obligated to attend a party might think, "This is an excellent opportunity to meet people and network!". This outlook will leave them looking forward to the event. Another person, who is less keen may think "I don't know most of the guests, so I just want to get it over and done with as quickly as possible". As you can see, it is not a situation itself that directly affects how people feel emotionally, but rather, our thoughts and perception about that situation.

When people are in distress, their perspectives and judgments are often clouded and inaccurate, causing their thoughts and imagination to run wild. CBT helps people identify thoughts that are causing them anxiety and evaluate how realistic the thoughts actually are when examined more closely. Patients then learn to change their distorted thinking patterns and adopt a more realistic approach.

(Chapter 5 continues in the full book)

Check out the rest of "Overcoming Anxiety - Practical Approaches You Can Use To Manage Fear & Anxiety In The Moment & Long Term" by me, Jane Aniston on the Amazon store!

Check Out My Other Books!

Understanding Anxiety - *Why You're Suffering From Anxiety & How You Can Start Breaking Free!*

Overcoming Anxiety - *Practical Approaches You Can Use To Manage Fear & Anxiety In The Moment & Long Term*

Depression - Practical & Natural Approaches You Can Use To Cure Depression In The Moment & Long Term

Cognitive Behavioral Therapy - A Practical Guide To C.B.T. For Overcoming Anxiety, Depression, Addictions & Other Psychological Conditions

Homemade Shampoo (Includes 34 Organic Shampoo Recipes!)

Homemade Makeup (Includes 28 Organic Makeup Recipes!)

Homemade Deodorant (Includes 20 Organic Deodorant Recipes!)

Homemade Lip Balm (Includes 22 Organic Lip Balm Recipes!)

Homemade Bath Salts (Includes 35 Organic Bath Salt Recipes!)

(All books available as digital downloads and printed books)